INVESTIGATING EARTH

FOSSIL INVESTIGATORS

BY REBECCA STORM

CONTENTS

Words in **BOLD** can be found in the glossary.

First published in 2025 by Hungry Tomato Ltd
F15, Old Bakery Studios, Blewetts Wharf, Malpas Road, Truro, Cornwall, TR1 1QH, UK.

A CIP catalog record for this book is available from the British Library.

ISBN 9781835693285

Manufactured in the USA

Discover more at
www.hungrytomato.com

Picture credits:
Abbreviations: m-middle, t-top, l-left, r-right, bg-background.

Graham Rich: 7(all). Chris and Helen Pellant: 12br. Shutterstock: 28tl; AlessandroZocc 5tl, 11tl; Alex Coan 14tl; AnnaRoth108 10br; Arjen de Ruiter 24mr; Bjoern Wylezich 8br, 26bl; bluehand 5m; Breck P. Kent 5br, 22mr; CatbirdHill 27bl; Danny Ye 6b; Denis---S 31tr; Doug McLean 23bl; Edgloris Marys 29bl; Elnur 17m; encierro 21mr; Faviel_Raven 24tl; frantic00 4t; Gorodenkoff 1bg, 16m; Guillermo Guerao Serra 22bl; Henri Koskinen 23mr; Jaroslav Moravcik 14mr; Jimmy Ryan 14bl; Keneva Photography 18t; krugloff 21br; Lacey Dent 29tl, 29mr; lev radin 11mr; Mark Brandon 12tl; Mark Godden 18b, 21ml; mark higgins 19t; Mark_Kostich 10tl; MISTER DIN 21tl; Mykoalastock 20b; Nancy Bauer 11bl; Natalia van D 23mr; ND700 22tl; Negrobov 26tl; netsuthep 9tr; Nick Greaves 9ml; paleontologist natural 16b; Pao W 28br; salajean 26mr; schusterbauer.com 13tl; Sergio Foto 31bl; servickuz 13mr; Ton Bangkeaw FC, 2-3bg, 30m; Rebus_Productions 23tl; Ryan M. Bolton 8ml; Viacheslav Lopatin 25tl; Victor1153 27mr; Vladimir Wrangel 24bl; Warpaint 6tr; Yes058 Montree Nanta 9br; Yes058 Montree Nanta 25bl, 27tl; Yuris C. Hassan 13bl; Zeyu pan 19b;

Every effort has been made to trace the copyright holders, and we apologize in advance for any unintentional omissions. We would be pleased to insert the appropriate acknowledgments in any subsequent edition of this publication.

WHAT ARE FOSSILS?

Plants and animals have lived on Earth for millions of years. Fossils are the shape or remains of plants and animals that lived long ago. Fossils are preserved in rock.

Fossils can form from **TINY SEA CREATURES** or **GIANT DINOSAURS!**

Often, fossils teach us about **PLANTS AND ANIMALS** that no longer exist, like T.rex and pterodactyls! Sometimes, we find fossils of things that do still exist. By comparing fossils with living things, we can see how they have changed, or not changed, over millions of years.

Some coelacanth fossils are more than 400 million years old. This type of fish still lives today, so we call it a **"LIVING FOSSIL"**.

COELACANTH FISH ALIVE

COELACANTH FISH FOSSIL

GINKGO TREES look very similar to how they looked 200 million years ago.

HOW DO FOSSILS FORM?

Very few of the animals and plants that lived on Earth millions of years ago have been fossilized. This is because fossils only form in special conditions.

To become a fossil, an animal or plant has to be **BURIED QUICKLY.** Otherwise, their bodies would rot away or be eaten before they had time to turn into fossils!

Nearly all the fossils we find are from animals that lived in the ocean, like shellfish and sharks. These animals were buried in sand or mud much quicker than land animals.

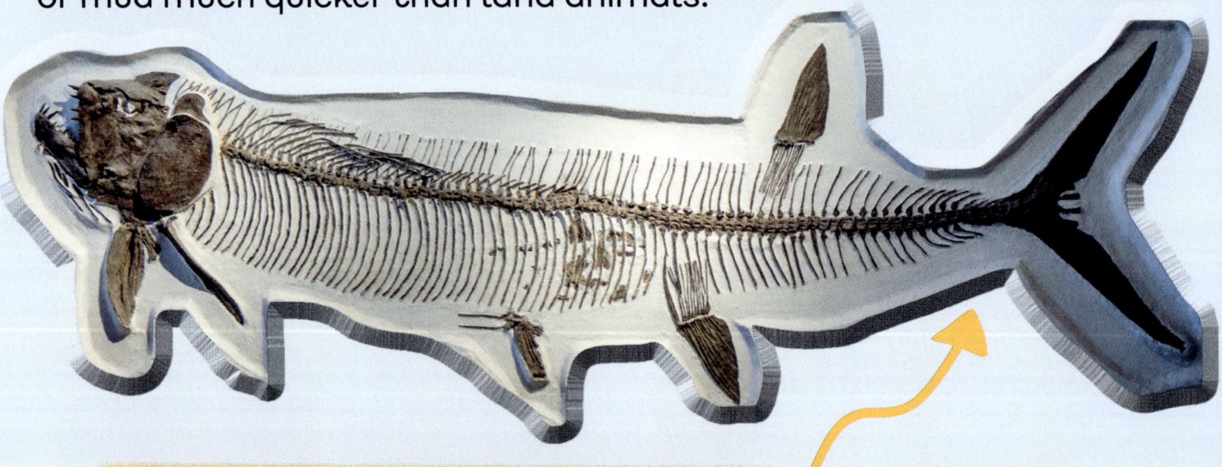

THE FOSSIL OF A PREHISTORIC FISH

HOW A SEA ANIMAL MIGHT BECOME FOSSILIZED:

1. The animal dies and its body sinks to the seafloor. The soft parts of its body quickly rot away.

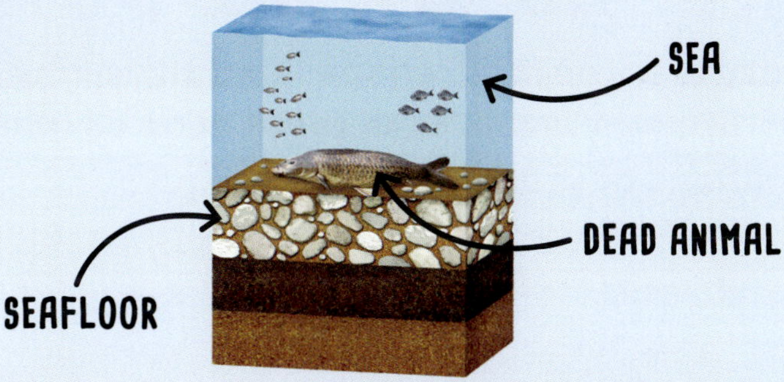

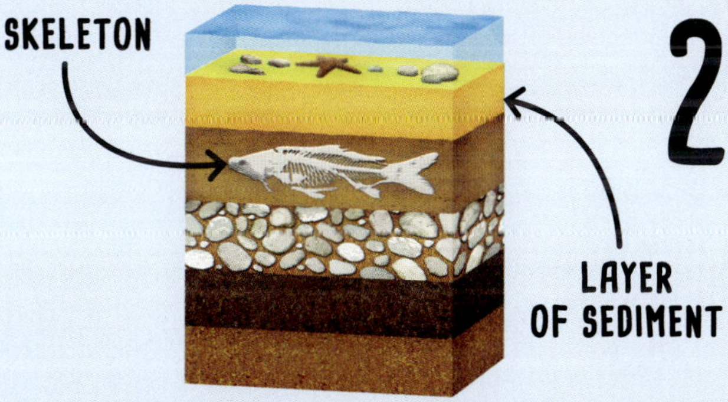

2. Its skeleton gets covered in tiny grains of rock called sediment. Under the sediment, the hard bits of the skeleton are replaced by **minerals**.

3. As more layers of sediment build up, their weight pushes down. This force turns the sediment grains into **sedimentary rock**, trapping the skeleton inside.

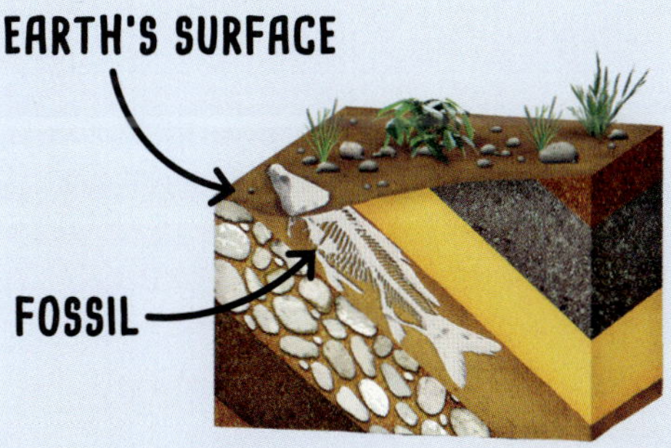

4. Movements under Earth's surface sometimes shift layers of rock upward. Weather, like wind and rain, wear away the rock and reveal the fossil.

TYPES OF FOSSILS

Fossils come in all shapes and sizes, and can be preserved in lots of different ways. Each fossil tells us about the things that lived millions of years ago.

TEETH AND BONES

The most common animal fossils are hard body parts, like teeth and bones, that have been protected in rock. Soft body parts, like skin and organs, rotted away really quickly, making **fossilization** of these parts almost impossible.

INSECTS IN AMBER

Sometimes insects get trapped in the sticky resin of pine trees. Over time, the resin hardens, turning into **amber** that perfectly preserves the insects.

FOOTPRINTS

When dinosaurs wandered across riverbanks, they left muddy footprints behind. As the mud dried, more layers of mud covered the footprints. These layers hardened, fossilizing the footprints.

SHELL CRYSTALS

Ammonites were shelled animals that used to live in the sea. Their shells are very common fossils. The shells are divided into small parts called chambers.

FOSSILIZED WOOD

It's not just animal fossils we find, but plant fossils too! As the wood slowly rotted, minerals replaced different parts of the plant. The wood may look the same, but now it's rock hard!

OCEAN FOSSILS

Earth is millions of years old, and is always changing. Some places that are on land today were once under the ocean! We know this because we have found fossils of ocean animals on land.

GIANT SHARK TEETH

Megalodons are thought to have been the biggest sharks ever. We only know about them because of their teeth fossils. Their teeth measure up to 7 inches (18 cm) long – that's almost 3 times the size of great white shark teeth!

CURIOUS CRINOIDS

Crinoids may be called "sea lillies", but they are actually sea creatures. Many of their fossils date back 300 million years. Some crinoid species still live in the ocean today, but they're not as big.

Mountainous Trilobites

Trilobites had hard shells and lived on the seafloor. Some had eyes on stalks to help them see when they were hidden under sand. Their fossils have been found on Mount Everest – the tallest mountain in the world (above sea level)!

Monstrous Mosasaurs

Scientists have found fossils of gigantic **reptiles** that lived in the ocean when dinosaurs walked on land. These predators, which included mosasaurs, plesiosaurs, and pliosaurs, grew bigger than many ocean predators today.

Ancient Brachiopods

One of the oldest animal fossils ever discovered, people have found brachiopod shells that are more than 540 million years old! They are some of the most common fossils of that time.

LAND FOSSILS

The **habitats** on Earth used to be very different from today. Fossils tell us what plants and animals were around, as well as information about the weather, climate, and natural disasters like volcanic eruptions!

EARLY BIRD?

Archaeopteryx was a major fossil find! A mix between a bird and a dinosaur, Archaeopteryx allowed scientists to show that birds are related to dinosaurs. It was covered in feathers, which hinted that many other dinosaurs may have been too.

SWAMPY MAYFLY

Mayflies are among the first winged insects that were able to fly! These animals only fossilized in very **fine** mud. This is how we know that the places they lived must have been muddy, like swamps or rivers.

GIGANTIC ANIMALS

Fossils show us that the dinosaurs that roamed Earth millions of years ago lived similarly to animals today, even if they looked different and were much bigger! Some, like titanosaurs, grew long necks to eat from the tops of tall trees.

FASCINATING FERNS

Because of fossil evidence, we know that fern-like plants that lived millions of years ago are similar to ferns that grow today, which helps us understand what landscapes looked like long ago.

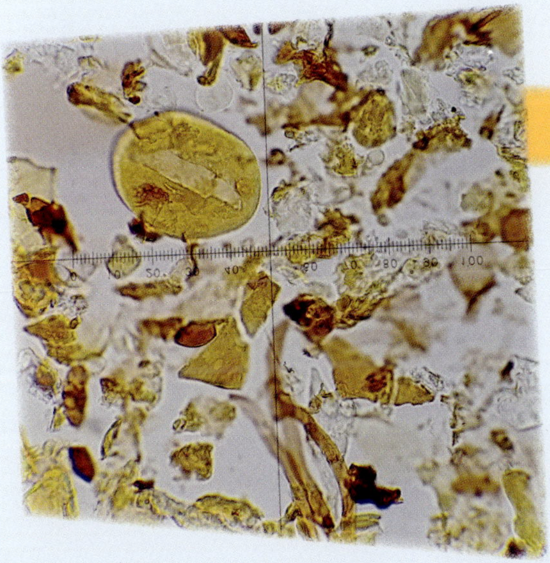

SUPRISING POLLEN

Pollen fossils give clues about the plants that used to live, even if no other parts of the plants have fossilized. Thanks to this, scientists have learned of a **mass extinction** of plants just before the dinosaurs lived!

WHAT CAN WE LEARN FROM FOSSILS?

All sorts of information can be uncovered from fossils. We have already seen some examples of what fossils teach us, but there's so much more to discover!

Fossils of **ANIMAL POOP**, and remains found inside animals' stomachs, have taught us what prehistoric animals used to eat!

The discovery of **FOSSILIZED NESTS FULL OF EGGS** help us understand how animals, like dinosaurs, gave birth to their babies.

Finding fossils in **BIG GROUPS** shows us which animals may have lived in herds, just like some wild animals do today.

All fossils are **dated** to work out how old they are. This means we can see which plants and animals lived at the same time. Scientists often use a timeline to show different times in history, which is broken up into **eras** and **periods**.

ERA	PERIOD	MILLION YEARS AGO
PALEOZOIC (pay-lee-uh-zoh-ick)	Cambrian	541
	Ordivician	485
	Silurian	444
	Devonian	419
	Carboniferous	359
	Permian	299
MESOZOIC (mess-uh-zoh-ick)	Triassic	252
	Jurassic	201
	Cretaceous	145
CENOZOIC (see-nuh-zoh-ick)	Paleogene	66
	Neogene	23
	Quaternary	2.6

FOSSIL DETECTIVES

Fossils are amazing and can help us unlock the past. But how do we know about them and the secrets they hold?

The scientists who study fossils are called **PALEONTOLOGISTS**. It's thanks to their studies that we have learned so much about fossils and the living things they came from.

Paleontologists spend lots of time on **dig sites**, looking for, and digging up, fossils. They have to be careful – fossils are very fragile, and they don't want to damage them. The scientists use **chisels** and brushes to gently remove rock and dirt from around fossils.

They also spend time in the **LAB**, doing tests on fossils to work out information like how old they are, what animal or plant they came from, and if what they've found is a new species. They use high-tech machines, including microscopes and scanners.

Paleontologists are making new discoveries all the time! Those who study dinosaurs think we've only found a tiny number of species, and that there may be **HUNDREDS MORE OUT THERE, WAITING TO BE DISCOVERED...**

AMAZING FOSSIL PLACES

Fossils have been found all over the world, but some places have many more fossils than others. Sometimes they are part of the landscape, so you don't have to go fossil hunting to see them!

PETRIFIED FOREST, USA

The Arizona desert in this picture is scattered with tree fossils. Even though it is a desert today, millions of years ago it was a forest!

JURASSIC COAST, UK

Fossils from the whole Mesozoic era have been found along the Jurassic coast, but it's best known for its amazing Jurassic fossils.

RIVERSLEIGH, AUSTRALIA

The remote outback of Riversleigh is rich in fossils. More than 200 previously unknown animal species have been uncovered there!

CHENGJIANG, CHINA

Many incredible fossils have been found in China, including at the Chengjiang fossil site where around 200 high-quality fossils have been uncovered.

HOW TO FIND FOSSILS

You don't have to be an expert to find fossils; you just need a few basic tools and to know what to look for!

TO GET STARTED, YOU WILL NEED:

- A backpack for carrying your finds
- Old towels and plastic bags to line your backpack
- Goggles to protect your eyes
- A geological hammer with a steel head
- A chisel for splitting rocks
- A soft brush for wiping away dust and dirt
- A magnifying glass
- A camera for taking pictures of fossils that are too big to carry
- A notebook and pencil for writing down your findings

BEFORE YOU GO

Plan your trip carefully. Some places have rules about collecting fossils – make sure you know the rules where you're going so you can follow them.

STAYING SAFE

Always go with an adult and stick together. Pack food, water, and a cell phone in case you need to call for help.

FINDING FOSSILS

Fossils are often found in sedimentary rock, such as **sandstone**, **limestone**, and **clay**. Sometimes fossils are on the surface of rocks. Other times, you may need to split rocks open to find fossils – always ask an adult to do this.

DISPLAYING YOUR FOSSILS

Fossils are fragile and cleaning them is difficult, so keep them away from dust. Make a tray to keep them in and use a piece of cardstock to write each fossil's name, age, and the place it was found.

PALEOZOIC FOSSILS

People have found so many incredible fossils. Here are some common finds from the Paleozoic era.

Trilobite paradoxides

- Period: Cambrian
- Found: North America and Europe
- Features: Large, hard-shelled sea creature with spines

Trilobite phacops

- Period: Silurian and Devonian
- Found: North America, Europe, and northern Africa
- Features: Hard-shelled sea creature with a rounded outline

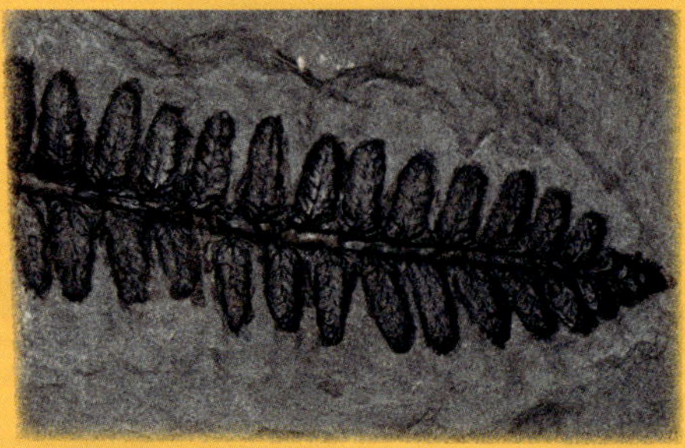

Pecopteris

- Period: Carboniferous
- Found: Europe, northern Africa, and Asia
- Features: Long, fern-like stems with lots of individual leaves

Brachiopod (Productus)

- Period: Devonian
- Found: Worldwide
- Features: Rounded, hard-cased shell with line details

Coral (Halysites)

- Period: Ordovician and Silurian
- Found: North America, Europe, Asia, and Australia
- Features: A type of coral that is linked together like a chain

Calamites

- Period: Carboniferous and Permian
- Found: Worldwide
- Features: Wide plant stems that grew to be very tall

MESOZOIC FOSSILS

There are lots of fossils in the world, just waiting to be found. Here are some common finds from the Mesozoic era.

Belemnites

- Period: Jurassic and Cretaceous
- Found: Europe
- Features: Pointed, tube-like structures that vary in size

Coral (Isastrea)

- Period: Jurassic and Cretaceous
- Found: North and South America, Europe, Asia, and Africa
- Features: Shell structures, similar in shape to modern-day limpets

Ammonite (Scaphites)

- Period: Cretaceous
- Found: Worldwide
- Features: Tight spiral shells, often ribbed and sometimes with bumps

Ichthyosaurs

- Period: Triassic, Jurassic, and Cretaceous
- Found: North and South America, Europe, Asia, and Australia
- Features: Large marine reptiles with long snouts and crescent tails

Bivalve (Pecten)

- Period: Cretaceous to Quaternary
- Found: Worldwide
- Features: Large, clam-like shapes

Maidenhair tree (Ginkgo)

- Period: Triassic to Quaternary
- Found: Worldwide
- Features: Wide leaves with thin stems

CENOZOIC FOSSILS

Searching for fossils is like being a prehistoric detective! Here are some common finds from the Cenozoic era.

MAMMOTH TUSK

- Period: Quaternary
- Found: North America, Europe, and Asia
- Features: Long brown and cream curved tusks, often with darker markings

SHARK TOOTH (LAMNA)

- Period: Cretaceous to Quaternary
- Found: Worldwide
- Features: Sharp, pointed teeth with bony ridge at the base

AMBER

- Period: Paleogene
- Found: Worldwide
- Features: Bright yellow or orange gems, sometimes with insects inside!

Plant leaf Acer (Maple)

- Period: Paleogene to Quaternary
- Found: Worldwide
- Features: Wide, pronged leaf, just like maple leaves today

Bear tooth (Ursus)

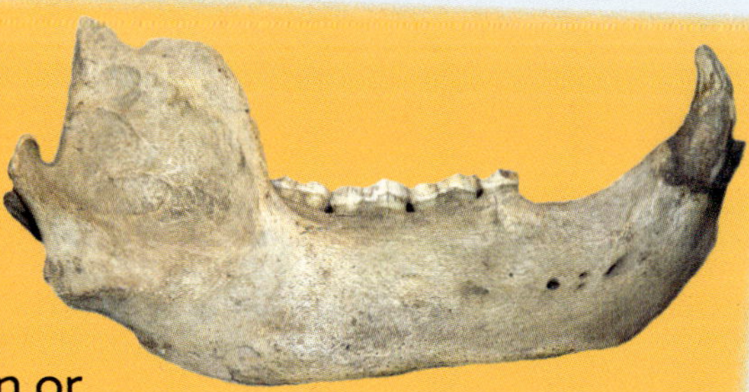

- Period: Quaternary
- Found: Europe and Asia
- Features: This is the canine tooth; they're long, and brown or cream with darker flecks!

Fish (Knightia)

- Period: Paleogene
- Found: North America and Asia
- Features: Small-to-medium sized bony fish

RECORD-BREAKING FOSSILS

Many amazing fossils have been found before, but these are some of the most impressive.

Some of the **OLDEST FOSSILS** ever found are 3.5 billion years old! They are the remains of **algae** that have been found in Western Australia.

THIS ROCK CONTAINS MILLIONS OF TINY FOSSILIZED ALGAE.

The **EARLIEST DINOSAUR FOSSIL** ever found belongs to the Herrerasaurus. It is thought to date back 233 million years!

THIS IS A REPLICA OF THE HERRERASAURUS.

The award for the **BIGGEST DINO TOOTH** goes to T.rex. The biggest fossil tooth from this meat-eater measured a mighty 12 inches (30 cm)!

SCARY T.REX TEETH!

Liverworts are some of the **FIRST PLANTS** that grew on land, and many species still grow today! The oldest fossils of liverworts are around 473 million years old!

MANY TYPES OF LIVERWORTS ARE GROWING ON EARTH TODAY.

The **BIGGEST ANIMAL SKULL** ever recorded belonged to a Torosaurus. This dinosaur's skull was 10 feet (3 m) long – the same as two park benches pushed together!

THIS IS A REPLICA OF THE TOROSAURUS SKULL.

TRUE OR FALSE?

There's lots to learn about fossils. How well do you know your fossil facts?

All fossils are more than 10,000 years old!

TRUE! To be called a fossil, the remains or impression of a living thing have to be older than 10,000 years old.

Scientists always find whole skeletons!

FALSE! It's very rare for scientists to find whole fossilized skeletons. Usually, they just find small parts, and have to use logic and computers to work out what it had looked like whole!

The dinosaurs were wiped out by an ice age!

FALSE! Fossil evidence suggests that 66 million years ago a huge asteroid crashed into Earth, wiping out almost all of the animals, including the dinosaurs! It seems only the smallest survived.

Scientists can work out how fast dinosaurs ran by looking at their footprints!

TRUE! From footprint fossils, scientists estimate the fastest dinosaur ran at speeds around 25 miles per hour (40 km).

GLOSSARY

Algae – plant-like organisms that live in water.

Amber – sap from trees that has hardened and fossilized. It's usually yellow or orange.

Chisels – long metal tools that are used to chip away solid material, like rock or wood.

Clay – a type of sedimentary rock (see right) that is very sticky when wet.

Crystals – a solid material that forms in a repeated pattern.

Dated (fossils) – to work out how old something is.

Dig sites – areas of land where something specific is being dug up.

Era - a length of time in the history of the Earth. Eras lasted tens of millions of years.

Fine (mud) – mud that is made of very small pieces of rock.

Fossilization – the process of something becoming a fossil.

Fossilized – something that has become a fossil.

Habitats – the place(s) where animals and plants live.

Limestone – a type of sedimentary rock (see below) made mainly of the mineral calcite, that forms in shells and corals. Limestone can contain fossils.

Mass extinction – an event where many of the world's plant and animal species are wiped out so that they no longer exist.

Minerals – substances that are naturally found in things like rocks, sand, and soil. Many minerals form as crystals.

Period – a length of time in the history of the Earth. Periods lasted millions of years. Many periods make up one era (see left).

Pollen – a fine powder produced by some plants to help them make new seeds.

Reptiles – a group of cold-blooded animals, including snakes, lizards, and dinosaurs.

Sandstone – a type of sedimentary rock (see below) made of grains of sand that have compacted together.

Sedimentary rock – a type of rock that is made of layers of sand or rock grains. The layers get pressed together and harden to form solid rocks.

INDEX